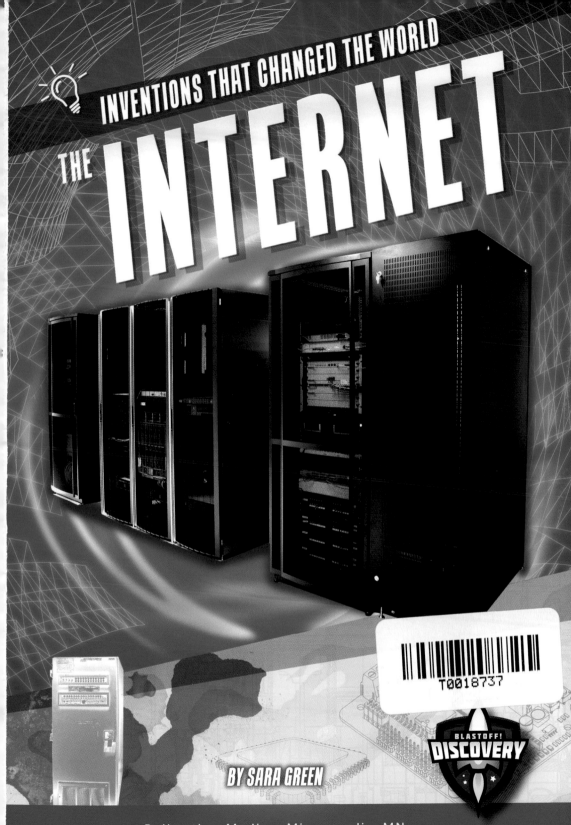

INVENTIONS THAT CHANGED THE WORLD

THE INTERNET

BY SARA GREEN

BLASTOFF! DISCOVERY

Bellwether Media • Minneapolis, MN

a new mission: reading to learn.
Filled with facts and features,
each book offers you an exciting
new world to explore!

BLASTOFF! UNIVERSE

BLASTOFF!
DISCOVERY

BLASTOFF!
Beginners

BLASTOFF!
READERS

GRADE
K

GRADES
1-3

GRADE
4

This edition first published in 2022 by Bellwether Media, Inc.

No part of this publication may be reproduced in whole or in part without
written permission of the publisher.
For information regarding permission, write to Bellwether Media, Inc.,
Attention: Permissions Department,
6012 Blue Circle Drive, Minnetonka, MN 55343.

Library of Congress Cataloging-in-Publication Data

LC record for The Internet available at: https://lccn.loc.gov/2021049246

Text copyright © 2022 by Bellwether Media, Inc. BLASTOFF! DISCOVERY
and associated logos are trademarks and/or registered trademarks of
Bellwether Media, Inc.

Editor: Rebecca Sabelko   Designer: Josh Brink

Printed in the United States of America, North Mankato, MN.

TABLE OF CONTENTS

INTERNET IN ACTION!

It is early morning. A family is sleeping. But devices around the house are buzzing with activity. The devices are connected to the Internet. It is powering them on!

Sprinklers pop up from the ground. They start watering the lawn. In the kitchen, the coffee maker brews coffee. The refrigerator sends an alert to the parents. They need more milk! Window shades rise in the bedrooms, and smart alarms ring. It is time for everyone to get up!

The Internet helps the family start its day. Smart bathroom mirrors display news updates as everyone gets ready. During breakfast, the parents' smartphones buzz. There is a traffic accident nearby. The smartphones suggest different routes to school and work.

The Internet locks the doors when the family leaves. It turns off the lights. A dog camera even tosses a treat to the family poodle. Later, the Internet will make the house warm and bright. Welcome home, family!

EARLY CONNECTIONS

The Internet is a worldwide system of computer **networks**. They communicate with one another at rapid speeds. Each computer in a network has its own **IP address**. Computers use it to send and receive information.

ARPANET network diagram

DID YOU KNOW?

The word "Internet" was introduced in 1974. It is short for "internetworking." It refers to cables and computers all connecting together.

INTERFACE MESSAGE PROCESSOR

Developed for the Advanced Research Projects Agency by Bolt Beranek and Newman Inc.

ARPANET router

During the **Cold War**, the United States government feared the **Soviet Union** could destroy communication lines. The government created a network called ARPANET to stop this from happening. ARPANET used **packet switching** to send messages between four computers. More networks were built in the 1970s. Machines called **routers** connected them. This system came to be known as the Internet.

TIM BERNERS-LEE

Born: June 8, 1955, in London, United Kingdom

Background: Computer scientist at CERN, a physics laboratory in Switzerland

Invented: World Wide Web

Year Invented/Released: Invented in 1989; introduced to the world in 1993

Idea Development: Scientists at CERN were having trouble sharing information with each other from their computers. Berners-Lee invented a way to link web pages using text and images.

DID YOU KNOW?

Tim Berners-Lee made it free to use the World Wide Web. This made the Web available to anyone who wanted to use it.

At first, mainly scientists used the Internet. But in the 1980s, sales of personal computers soared. Many people began using the Internet to send emails, read news, and share information.

In the early 1990s, Tim Berners-Lee introduced the **World Wide Web**, or the Web. The Web is a collection of linked web pages found on the Internet. It gives users easy access to the network. Web **browsers** help people find and view web pages. Early browsers included Mosaic and Netscape Navigator. Today, Chrome, Safari, and Edge are widely used.

Netscape Navigator

Web surfing became a daily activity in the 1990s. The rise of **search engines** such as Yahoo! helped boost the Internet's popularity. In 1995, the U.S. government shifted control of the Internet to businesses. The number of websites skyrocketed from one in 1991 to more than 17 million in 2000!

DID YOU KNOW?

The search engine Google was launched in 1998 by Larry Page and Sergey Brin. Today, it is the most popular search engine in the world!

People used dial-up **modems** and phone lines to connect to the Internet. Connection speeds were slow. A single web page could take over two minutes to load. Still, the Internet gave people access to a lot of information!

GROWTH AND CHANGE

Internet technology continued to improve. In the early 2000s, an Internet connection called **broadband** began replacing dial-up. Broadband is faster. Popular types include cable, wireless, and fiber. Fiber is the fastest. Information travels along thin fibers at lightning speeds!

broadband cabinet

The growth of **Wi-Fi** technology allowed people to use devices without plugging in. Wi-Fi uses **radio waves** to connect devices to routers. Wi-Fi **hotspots** began popping up in public places such as airports and coffee shops. Today, more than 22 billion devices are connected to Wi-Fi!

Wi-Fi uses radio waves to send signals to other devices. **Internet Service Providers**, or ISPs, connect devices to Wi-Fi and allow devices to send and receive information. They also give every connected device its own IP address.

Information is too large to send in one piece. It is sent through the Internet in small packets. Each packet is linked to an IP address. Routers read the address and send the packets to the correct device. When the packets arrive, the information is put back together. This is what shows up on a screen. This entire process happens in less than a second!

DID YOU KNOW?

Internet information flows through underground wires and cables around the world. Long cables running beneath the oceans connect continents together!

underground
fiber optic cables

HOW IT WORKS

WI-FI

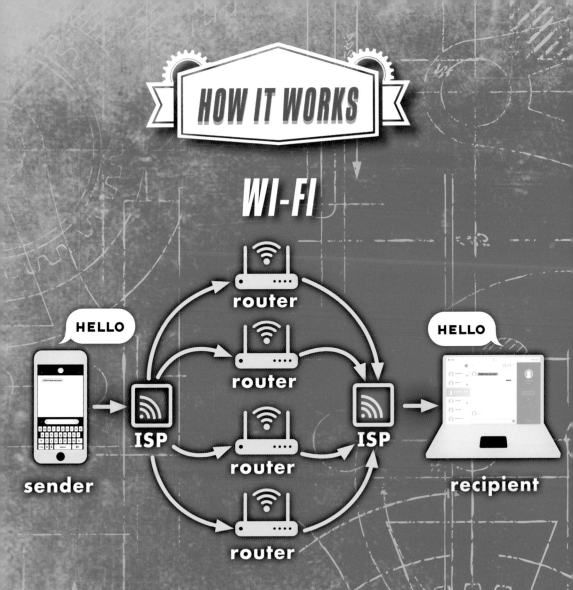

A message sent over Wi-Fi travels through radio waves. The message breaks into packets and travels through the ISP to routers. The routers use the information to send the message to the recipient's ISP. The recipient's ISP delivers the information to the recipient's device. The message is put back together!

GLOBAL CONNECTIONS

Today, more than half the world's population has access to the Internet. Many people use it daily to search for information, shop, and communicate with others. Social media websites allow users to do many of these things in one place. YouTube, Instagram, and Facebook are favorites!

Smartphones allow users to access the Internet from almost anywhere. **Apps** have exploded in popularity with the rise of mobile devices. Users can play games, watch videos, or listen to music almost anytime they want!

DID YOU KNOW?

In 2019, the average person spent almost two and a half hours each day using social media. Today, around 3 billion people have at least one social media account.

apps

POPJAM

Inventor's Name: Mind Candy

Year of Release: 2014

Uses: PopJam is an online community of kids between the ages of 7 and 12. Users create and share art, take quizzes, and connect with other kids.

The Internet of Things, or IoT, is also growing. IoT devices are connected to the Internet and to other devices. They communicate and share information with each other.

IoT technology is often used in cities. It can monitor traffic, manage bridges, and measure river water levels. The IoT is also useful at home. People can control televisions, lightbulbs, and refrigerators from their smartphones or computers. Today, there are more objects connected to the Internet than there are people on Earth!

Connected vehicles take the Internet on the road. Owners can use apps to operate their cars **remotely**. They can unlock doors, start engines, and honk horns. Connected vehicles will even call for help in case of an emergency!

DID YOU KNOW?

Mount Everest is the world's highest mountain. It is also one of the most remote places on Earth. Even so, people climbing Mount Everest can connect to the Internet as they climb!

START
ENG

remote learning

The Internet is also an important part of the school day. Kids can learn remotely, submit homework online, and receive instant feedback from their teachers. The Internet offers exciting **virtual** experiences, too. Visits to museums, historic sites, cities, and countries are easy online!

The Internet has many great uses, but it also poses risks. Some material may be unsafe for kids. **Cyberbullies** use the Internet to hurt others. **Cybercriminals** try to steal money or personal information.

False news and information can mislead people into believing things that are not true. Sometimes, adults pretend to be kids online. They may try to put kids into unsafe situations. Kids should only make online contact with people they know. This helps them stay safe on the Internet.

A WIRELESS FUTURE

The Internet is likely to grow in exciting ways. Smart bed sheets may track sleep patterns. Smart clothing may monitor people's heart rates and temperatures. It could warn them of possible health problems. Smart clothes might also send, receive, and display messages one day!

smart clothing

Neuralink brain chip concept

Brain chips are also being studied. These chips may allow users to connect to the Internet with only their thoughts. The Internet changed how people live, work, and play across the planet. Who knows how much further it will go!

INTERNET TIMELINE

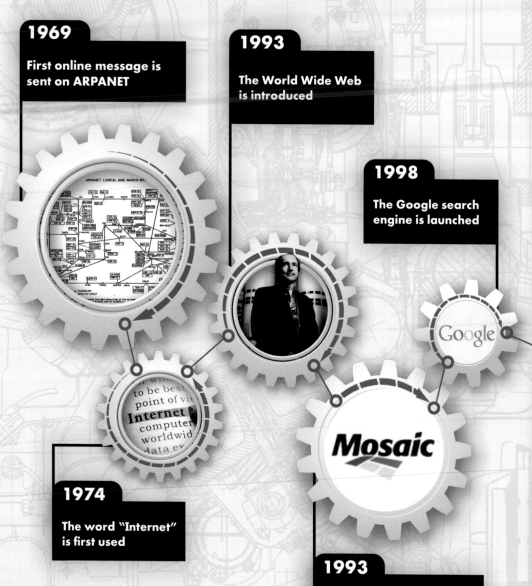

1969

First online message is sent on ARPANET

1993

The World Wide Web is introduced

1998

The Google search engine is launched

1974

The word "Internet" is first used

1993

Mosaic, the first popular web browser available to the public, is launched

2004

Facebook goes online as TheFacebook

2007

The first iPhone is released, making mobile Internet access more common

2022-

Future developments

2005

YouTube is launched

2019

More than 4 billion people are online

GLOSSARY

apps—computer programs that perform special functions

broadband—a high-speed electronic network that carries more than one type of communication

browsers—programs used to access the World Wide Web

Cold War—a long period of tension between the United States and the Soviet Union after 1945

cyberbullies—people who use the Internet to bully others

cybercriminals—people who use the Internet to commit crimes

hotspots—places where people can access the Internet through wireless connections

Internet Service Providers—companies that provide Internet access and services such as email accounts

IP address—a set of characters used to identify a device on a computer network

modems—devices that send and receive computer information over telephone lines, cables, or satellite connections

networks—groups of connected computers that operate together

packet switching—a way of sending information on the Internet in which the information is broken into small parts and then put back together at the endpoint

radio waves—invisible waves used to send signals through the air without using wires

remotely—from a distance

routers—computers that move information between computer networks using the shortest paths possible

search engines—types of websites that help computer users find information on the Internet

Soviet Union—short for the Union of Soviet Socialist Republics; the Soviet Union is a former country in Eastern Europe and western Asia made up of 15 republics or states that broke up in 1991.

virtual—happening through use of the Internet rather than in the physical world

Wi-Fi—a way for a computer to connect to a computer network using radio waves instead of wires

World Wide Web—a part of the Internet where users click links to move from page to page

TO LEARN MORE

AT THE LIBRARY

Amstutz, Lisa J. *Internet of Things*. Lake Elmo, Minn.: Focus Readers, 2020.

Beevor, Lucy. *The Invention of the Computer*. North Mankato, Minn.: Capstone Press, 2018.

Smibert, Angie. *The Internet*. Lake Elmo, Minn.: Focus Readers, 2018.

ON THE WEB

FACTSURFER

Factsurfer.com gives you a safe, fun way to find more information.

1. Go to www.factsurfer.com.

2. Enter "Internet" into the search box and click 🔍.

3. Select your book cover to see a list of related content.

INDEX

The images in this book are reproduced through the courtesy of: improvise, front cover (hero); Steve Jurvetson/ Wiki Commons, front cover (small), p. 9; CG_dmitriy, front cover (microchip left); Andrii Stepaniuk, front cover (motherboard right); Gorodenkoff, p. 4; Subbotina Anna, p. 5; aslysun, pp. 6-7, 20-21; Archive PL/ Alamy, pp. 8-9; dpa picture alliance/ Alamy, p. 10; ASSOCIATED PRESS/ AP Images, p. 11 (Netscape screen); S. Vincent/ Alamy, p. 11 (computer); Kim Kulish/ Getty Images, p. 12; parkerphotography/ Alamy, p. 13; David J. Green/ Alamy, p. 14; Heorshe/ Alamy, p. 15; Maren Winter/ Alamy, p. 16; Rebecca Sabelko/ Bellwether Media, p. 18; Nuchylee, p. 18 (cell phone right); Issac Johnson, p. 19 (cell phone); Elizabeth Neuenfeldt/ Bellwether Media, p. 19 (cell phone screen); dolgachov/ Alamy, p. 22; Jochen Tack/ Alamy, p. 23; CGN089, p. 24; fizkes, p. 25; Jeff Fitlow/ AP Images, p. 26; JL Stock, p. 27; The Computer History Museum/ Wiki Commons, p. 28 (ARPANET); Feng Yu, p. 28 (word "Internet"); Justin Leighton/ Alamy, p. 28 (Web introduced); Pavel Kapysh, p. 28 (Mosaic); jejim, p. 28 (Google); fyv6561, p. 29 (Facebook); Alexey Boldin, p. 29 (YouTube); marleyPug, p. 29 (iPhone); Prostock-studio, p. 29 (online); Syda Productions, p. 29 (future).